Transformation 2020 Companion Journal

Edited by Elizabeth B. Hill, MSW and Jaime L. Williams

Foreword by Dr. Davia H. Shepherd

Written by Jacqueline A. Baldwin, Kacey Cardin, Maryann Cruz, Dee DiFatta, Lynn Gallant, Donna Martire Miller, Melissa Molinero, Lori Raggio, Kristi H. Sullivan, and Noelymari Sanchez Velez

A Ladies' Power Lunch Transformation Anthology Publication

GREEN HEART LIVING PRESS

Transformation 2020 Companion Journal

ISBN (paperback): 978-0-9991976-9-1

DEDICATION

for you, dear one,
may writing set you free

Table of Contents

How To Use This Book

There are many ways to use this book. No way is wrong. Here are some ideas.

- **Create a morning or evening writing routine** - Build a writing routine with the questions in this journal serving as a springboard for a daily journaling practice.

- **Be random** - Flip through the pages and pick any page that catches your eyes to respond to.

- **Create a 12-day writing adventure** - For twelve days, set aside time each day to respond to one of the twelve sections of the book.

- **Reading and reflection experience** - Read the corresponding chapter in *Transformation 2020*, then follow up with the questions in this journal by the same author.

- **Allow this to be part of a meditation or prayer practice** - Before beginning or after completing writing, allow space for meditation or prayer.

- **Create a discussion group** - Use the questions in this journal to invoke discussion, reflection, and loving support for you and your friends.

- **Devour it.** Sit down and read the whole thing. Why not?

Foreword: Burnout to Brilliance

Dr. Davia H. Shepherd

As women, especially women in business, we often feel as though we are alone.

I know I have felt that way.

We may feel as though we have to do it all ourselves and that struggle and hustle are the only path to success.

Words do not teach, but stories teach in a truly memorable way.

After my personal brush with burnout, I'm here to share that there is another, in my opinion better, way.

I love the opportunity to share my experiences with the hope that it may encourage anyone who is going through a tough time right now.

I share my story, with an intention to rally us as women to come together, to use the considerable resources that we have among us collectively so that we can all, not just survive, but also thrive.

Take a minute to tune in to your emotions in this moment. What is one thing that is happening in your life now that is less than ideal, and how could you reframe what is going on from a positive rather than negative perspective?

What are five things that are going well for you right now? It could be something as simple as being warm on a cold day, or as amazing as spending quality time with loved ones. Explain why you feel the way you feel.

Think about your day today and how it might unfold. Make short notes about how you would like each segment to proceed. Also note how you want to feel as you go through each segment (e.g., "As I get ready for work I want to be efficient and on time," or " I want to feel excited for the day ahead as I go through my morning routine").

"Because I'm practicing every day to maintain my inner peace, on the days when I need it the most I'll be able to weather the storm."
Dr. Davia H. Shepherd

Brilliance

About Davia

Dr. Davia H. Shepherd spends her days treating her patients, however her true passion is being a master connector. She is a certified retreat leader, a "recovering researcher," and she celebrates almost 2 decades in various areas of healthcare. She loves public speaking and is an international speaker and best selling author. She believes that women can live the best version of their lives in every area: Health, business, finances, relationships etc. She leads transformational retreats, conferences and free "Ladies' Power Lunch" events that focus on this ideal. Davia lives in Connecticut with her husband Wayne, her beloved children Preston and Christian, and her mom Phyllis.

Find Davia at www.LadiesPowerLunch.com

Brilliance

Love

1. Loving Forgiveness

Dee DiFatta

Who or what circumstances have you allowed to define you and/or deter you from living your deepest desires?

What are some limiting beliefs and self-doubts you learned or inherited growing up that are no longer serving you?

What would your life look like if you could lovingly forgive yourself and move forward without blame, shame, guilt, and resentment?

Forgiveness

"Do not allow your circumstances to define you."
Dee DiFatta

Forgiveness

Why Dee Wrote

Life doesn't always work out the way you plan, but you get to CHOOSE how to deal with it. Growing up, I was not aware of this. I allowed myself to be defined by my circumstances. I was always trying to "Fit In" so I could find love, acceptance, and validation from others. But I never realized until recently that everything I was seeking from the material world existed within me. I was born worthy, deserving, empowered, and loved. I just had to slow down in order to stop blocking these blessings. I have forgiven myself for not knowing what I know now. And this has liberated me from the inside out. It's time to stop surviving and start thriving!

About Dee

Dee DiFatta is a Perspective and PositiviDee coach, inspirational speaker, educator, and author. After 49 years of life, 27 years living with Multiple Sclerosis, and 17 years working full-time for someone else, Dee has taken her power back. She has set herself free by telling her story with authenticity.

Find Dee at: www.adoseofpositividee.com
dee@adoseofpositividee.com
https://www.facebook.com/deedifatta/

Forgiveness

Forgiveness

Forgiveness

2. The Journey Back To Me

Melissa Molinero

"Sometimes, in the quiet, when I think of my past or look in the mirror, I can still see the physical, emotional, and mental scars that shaped my view of the world before I could understand or even verbalize it."

What are things in your past that still haunt you today? What trauma have you run from that still slaps you in the face from time to time?

What are these things holding you back from? What breakthrough would be waiting for you on the other side of this past trauma if you did the work to let it go?

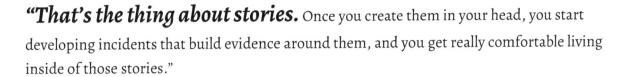

"*That's the thing about stories.* Once you create them in your head, you start developing incidents that build evidence around them, and you get really comfortable living inside of those stories."

What stories about yourself are you currently hiding behind? Examples: "Not worth it." "Not good enough." "Too ugly." "Too shy." "Not the right person."

The more you feed that story, the more it will become your reality. So, how long will you hide behind it? What would changing that story here and now take? And, what doors would open for you if you took that step?

"*When I finally surrendered* my life to God and took a chance on myself, realizing I was worth much more than I ever believed, my healing began. The breakthroughs leading to my transformation have been endless since."

Right now, in your current life, career, goals, etc., does the idea of surrendering scare you?

What are you trying to control that may be holding you back from getting all you really want?

What would taking one step in loosening your grip toward surrender bring you closer to?

"When I finally surrendered my life to God and took a chance on myself, realizing I was worth much more than I ever believed, my healing began. The breakthroughs leading to my transformation have been endless since."
Melissa Molinero

Acceptance

About Melissa

Melissa Molinero is a strong Christian woman with unwavering faith in God. She is a mom to two beautiful children who mean the world to her, a wife of 13 years to the most supportive and loving husband, and an ordained deacon at Woodcliff Community Reformed Church in North Bergen, New Jersey.

A life and career coach and certified job counselor in the state of New Jersey, Melissa offers individual and group coaching sessions, workshops, and professional résumé writing services. Melissa enjoys singing, reading, writing, community service, nature getaways, and creating events in service of personal growth and leadership development.

Find Melissa at www.msmcoaching.com

Acceptance

Acceptance

Acceptance

3. Putting the Pieces Together
Lynn Gallant

Many of us harbor insecurities about ourselves, physical or otherwise. Reflect on one or more of these and write a note to yourself expressing forgiveness, empathy, and compassion, as you would a dear friend.

Wholeness

Everyone has pieces of their past they may look back on and regret. Recall one of those moments or periods in your own life and write about it as an important part of who you are - it may have changed you, challenged you, or completed you.

Wholeness

When you think of the word wholeness as it relates to your life, describe the pieces of your life that make YOU feel WHOLE.

Wholeness

"It takes a village, and wholeness is never about just one thing. It's about the pieces coming together."

Lynn Gallant

Wholeness

About Lynn

Lynn Gallant is on a path to help create whole body wellness. A life balanced with good nutrition, positivity, self-care, movement and community is one that is full of goodness. Integrating healthy lifestyle changes, one at a time, is a great way to shift into wholeness. She is certified in health, nutrition and fitness and uses her platforms to implement whole food nutrition and fresh aeroponic greens to elevate gut and brain health.

Collaboration, connection, and community are priorities in her life and she is active in a number of amazing communities, one of which brought her to write this book.

Find Lynn at: www.lynngallant.com

Wholeness

Wholeness

Wholeness

4. Ignite the Fire Within

Noelymari Sanchez Velez

What are your current struggles with yourself?

Visualize exactly what you want to accomplish. Write these down. Be honest with yourself and do not feel shame in whatever these are.

Ignite

What is stopping you from igniting the fire within and taking a shot? What is the first step you will take to start YOUR own journey?

"When you have trusted the journey you have taken and are prepared to continue to DO the work, you will find opportunities to help others along the way."
Noelymari Sanchez Velez

Ignite

Why Noely Wrote

I shared my story in the Transformation 2020 book because I felt compelled to have my voice heard. I thought about why the reader might have picked up a book with such an inspirational title - it is because they are in search of a transformation. Like me, they might be struggling to make a decision on how to move forward, how to decide what to do next, to quiet a fear within and take the necessary steps to work on the best version of themselves.

We are our worst critics and it is human nature to compare ourselves to others, to think that others have it easier. We all struggle, we all fight with ourselves daily and it is not until we find the courage to ignite that fire within that we know we are not alone. It is my hope that you have felt inspired and moved to take the next step to transform your life, to live your best life.

About Noely

Noelymari Sanchez Velez works with her husband, Julio, as owners of JCV Freelance Photography, LLC, based out of East Hartford, CT. She and her husband engage in a healthy lifestyle by staying active along with sharing a mutual love for photography and chasing sunsets. It is Noely's passion to encourage and motivate others and to help them realize what they are capable of accomplishing.

Find Noely at: www.jcv-pics.com

Ignite

Ignite

Ignite

Emerge

5. The Unknown is Not the Enemy
Lori Raggio

Please sit quietly with your eyes closed. Pay attention to your breathing. Listen to your heart and soul as you answer these questions.

During this time in your life what are you being called to do, who are you being called to be?

What is currently preventing you from moving forward toward your calling? What fears are holding you back?

If anything and everything were possible, what is one step you could take today that would move you closer to your calling, to what is most important to you now?

Essence

"Without practices and rituals in place, our fears suck us back into our comfort zone, robbing us of what our soul desires."

Lori Raggio

Essence

Why Lori Wrote

I was called to share my transformation from control and perfectionism to surrender, trust, and faith at this time of a devastating global pandemic, massive destruction to mother earth, heightened racial injustice, and a collective pause.

I am hopeful that women leaders and entrepreneurs like you can identify with, learn from, feel supported and be inspired by my story so that you too can take actions that will lead you outside of your comfort zone and create a life that you desire and deserve. I also wanted to share my story now so that I can be more vulnerable and visible and continue my spiritual growth while being a catalyst for others.

About Lori

Lori Raggio, CEO, Inspire Greatness Coaching and Consulting serves as the creation catalyst and soul activist helping women leaders remove their armor, find their authentic self, and live aligned with their passion and purpose. She is powered by purpose, driven by insatiable curiosity, and guided by Source to impact the world.

Find Lori at lori@inspiregreatnesscoaching.com

Essence

Essence

Essence

Power

6. The Victor All Along

Jacqueline A. Baldwin

Have there been times or events in your life that have rendered you incapacitated for a time? What happened that allowed you to get moving again?

Victor

Do you have "scars" from your past? How do they appear to you today? Are they wounds that have not fully healed? Are they heavy reminders of the pain that inflicted them? Are you able to see them as reminders of the victories you have won?

Victor

What would you say your superpower is and why? Are there events you can point to that illuminated your superpower to you?

Victor

"I choose to see my scars not as wounds that did not heal completely but rather as reminders of the victories I have won."
Jacqueline A. Baldwin

Why Jacqueline Wrote

As is the case for so many women in this world, I had been filled with feelings of unworthiness, self-doubt and fear. Fear of not being loved, fear of not being good enough, fear of not doing enough good work to take away the guilt and shame of events from my past. At 55 years old, I can honestly say I had never experienced the complete peace and joy that dwells in my soul today until very recently. I finally have been able to release fear from my life and live in abundance. I desire for women existing in a life where fear takes up residence in their soul to be empowered to kick fear out forever and to find their super power hidden within.

About Jacqueline

As a financial advisor, Jacqueline is passionate about eradicating financial vulnerability. Her specialty is advising women who feel financially unprepared for the big what if's in life so they can feel confident knowing they have solutions for weathering any kind of storm.

Find Jacqueline at www.blfinarc.com

Victor

Victor

Victor

7. Hot Mess to Goddess
Kacey Cardin, PCC

Recall the childhood experiences that formed your core beliefs about yourself and the world. How do those beliefs impact your life today?

What does the author's perspective bring up for you around gender stereotypes and how they impact self-esteem?

Goddess

What paradigm-shifting experiences have occurred in your life, and how can they continue to shape you into a more empowered, loving version of yourself?

Goddess

"Fear builds walls. Love honors boundaries."
Kacey Cardin

Goddess

Why Kacey Wrote

Sharing our stories and what we've learned from them is cathartic for both the author and the reader. Until this anthology, I had not shared my story in writing publicly. I've been an outspoken advocate for sexual assault awareness for many years, and I have shared part of my story at various events, protests, and on podcasts, but I felt called to put into writing the transformation that was catalyzed by trauma. I believe most humans experience some form of trauma, and I also believe that what we choose to learn and create from its impact is part of our purpose. I hope that my story will provide education, entertainment, and perhaps access to more enlightenment for those who have struggled with their own version of the events I've documented.

About Kacey

Kacey Cardin, ACCC, PCC, is an Executive and Leadership Coach, facilitator, and trainer whose work has impacted leaders at companies including Google, Etsy, ABC, Fox, and Chief. Passionate about integrative leadership, Kacey created and presented a Tedx Talk on her framework called the 7 Wheels of Leadership and the concept of Energetic Intelligence for coaches and leaders. Her workshops and keynotes have been presented at Vanderbilt University, CreativeMornings, Conference for a Cause, and the Country Music Association, among others. A former opera singer who also studied energy healing for over 20 years, Kacey fused chakra balancing, burlesque, and coaching into a wellness class called Chakralesque. She specializes in coaching leaders who struggle with Imposter Syndrome and the "not enoughs", helping them create an authentic, fully expressed life and career. She resides in New York City and Nashville, and maintains a global private practice.

Find Kacey at www.kaceycardincoaching.com / www.chakralesque.com

Goddess

Goddess

Goddess

Success

8. Essentials for Your Transformation POTION

Maryann Cruz

Take a moment to think of what a successful life looks and feels like for you. How do YOU define success?

Passion

In thinking of transformation, what would you like to transform in your life?

Passion

Close your eyes for a few minutes. Clear your mind and ask yourself, "What is holding me back from success and transformation? What resources and/or tools do I need?"

Passion

"Be open-minded and optimistic, and opportunities will overflow."
Maryann Cruz

Passion

Why Maryann Wrote

I believe that the universe brings people together to inspire one another, strengthen the creative spirit, and positively impact the world.

In learning about the Transformation 2020 anthology, the vision, and getting a gentle nudge from another co-author, I knew the timing was right. Life is full of options and it's essential for others to know that their transformational journey and ingredients for success (the transformation POTION) will be unique to them.

About Maryann

Maryann Cruz is a business strategist and coach as well as co-founder of C3 Collaborative, LLC. Maryann assists creatives and passionate entrepreneurs gain clarity and momentum in business through the development of thorough strategies, action plans, and accountability. Maryann is an entrepreneur's co-pilot to success.

Find Maryann at www.maryanncruz.co

Passion

Passion

Passion

9. Aligned by Design
Kristi H. Sullivan

For much of our lives, starting when we are young, we receive social conditioning from our family (sometimes passed down through many generations) and other influencers, such as teachers, authority figures, advertising spokespersons, and celebrities. Consider the conditioning and related beliefs (perhaps even self-limiting) that you have learned and experienced in your life – inventory anything related to education, work, habits, attitudes, and life in general.

Design

According to Human Design, the head is meant for simply receiving information rather than complex decision making. Instead, we should connect to our intuition, gut-feelings and emotions in the body to help us tap into our deeper wisdom. Explore how you usually make decisions and the process as well as results when using your mind–compare this to the process and results when using your body-centric wisdom, and how you might tap more into this kind of decision making.

Design

Getting out of the head and into the body is critical for tapping into the wisdom that exists outside of the mind and deep within oneself. To access this, daily self-care activity is essential. Start by doing an assessment of your current self-care routine and habits—then determine what you need and how you can commit to making it a priority, not only for well-being but for helping to align your energy on a daily basis.

"Unlearning our conditioning and living in an unconditioned way is a new formula, and to do so is a daily practice and takes consistent self-care."
Kristi H. Sullivan

Design

Why Kristi Wrote

My journey with Human Design has led to one of my biggest, most recent transformations. The theory of Human Design is not widespread or mainstream (yet), so I hope that by sharing my story, others will realize the potentially life-altering shifts that can come from authentically living your best life by aligning to your true design. This directly ties to the ability we all have to manifest using energy alignment. I hope to inspire others to discover the effortless ability to create and attract more abundance and success in all areas of their lives!

About Kristi

Kristi Sullivan is a Wellness Advocate and Human Design Expert on a mission to help busy women give themselves permission to make self-care a priority and curate daily rituals so they can manifest abundance and live their best life in alignment with their true design.

Find Kristi at www.kristisselfcare.com, follow @KristiHSullivan on Instagram, or join her group on Facebook: Kristi's Self Care Tribe.

Design

Design

Design

Inspire(d)

10. Seven Transformation Stages to the Divine Feminine
Donna Martire Miller MA, CIPP

What propels you forward?

Divine

Whose love do you always carry with you?

What gift do you wish to share?

Divine

"Let's re-envision a world where we can transform suffering to the higher emotions of love, compassion and kindness.
A joy filled, juicy life worth living!"
Donna Martire Miller

Divine

Why Donna Wrote

I decided to share my story because transformation is important to recognize. We can start out with good goals or intentions and still get tossed around by people and problems that require us to change. It can be scary and very difficult. Many times we get mired down in the problem for way too long. We can judge ourselves harshly. Transformation helps us to move forward to stop blocking the blessings just waiting to befall us! In transformation, the possibilities are endless. We are always more than we can imagine. Our potential is bigger than our pain!

About Donna

Donna is an international keynote speaker and presenter. She is a professor of wellness and happiness. She is the owner of Happily Ever Actions, a business that applies cutting edge research to actions that help people to live their best life. She is considered an expert in strength-based living.

Find Donna at Donna@happilyeveractions.com

Divine

Divine

Divine

About Green Heart Living

Green Heart Living's mission is to make the world a more loving and peaceful place, one person at a time. Green Heart Living Press publishes inspirational books and stories of transformation, making the world a more loving and peaceful place, one book at a time.

Whether you have an idea for an inspirational book and want support through the writing process - or your book is already written and you are looking for a publishing path - Green Heart Living can help you get your book out into the world.

You can meet Green Heart authors on the Green Heart Living YouTube channel and the Green Heart Living podcast.

About Elizabeth B. Hill, MSW

Elizabeth B. Hill is CEO and founder of Green Heart Living. She is the best-selling author and publisher of *The Great Pause: Blessings and Wisdom from COVID-19*, *Love Notes: Daily Wisdom for the Soul* and *Green Your Heart, Green Your World: Avoid Burnout, Save the World and Love Your Life*.

Elizabeth coaches clients on mindful leadership and writing to heal, inspire, and grow their impact in the world. Trained as a social worker, yoga teacher, and ontological coach, she weaves creativity, spirituality, and mindfulness into her work with clients. With over 15 years of experience writing and leading collaborations in the nonprofit sphere, Elizabeth brings a uniquely engaging approach to collaborative book projects. Elizabeth lives in a matriarchal palace in Connecticut with her family and the neighborhood bears.

www.greenheartliving.com

Upcoming Collaborative Projects

Redefining Masculinity

Ladies' Power Lunch Transformation Anthology: Success in Any Season

Finding My Marbles with Bloom23 Productions

Embrace Your Space with Embrace Your Space CT

To apply to contribute to an upcoming collaboration,
or to publish an inspirational book of your own, go to
www.greenheartliving.com

Green Heart Living Publications

Transformation 2020: A Ladies' Power Lunch Transformation Anthology

The Great Pause: Blessings & Wisdom from COVID-19

The Great Pause Journal

Love Notes: Daily Wisdom for the Soul

Green Your Heart, Green Your World: Avoid Burnout,
Save the World and Love Your Life

Made in the USA
Coppell, TX
17 December 2020